02 The first computers

It's hard to imagine, but in 1945, the very first computer took up a whole room! It didn't have a monitor or a keyboard. Instead, people gave the computer instructions by changing wires.

1940s 1970s

Pixels and Coding

Contents

1	Computers are everywhere!	2
2	The first computers	4
3	What do computers do?	6
4	What we put in	8
5	What we get back	10
6	A computer's job	12
7	A computer's memory	14
8	Bits and binary	16
9	Pictures are pixels	18
10	Algorithms and code	20
11	Saving files	22
12	What is the internet?	24
13	Being safe on the internet	26
14	Computers in the future	28
	How computers work	30

Written by Jeannie Moulton

Collins

01 Computers are everywhere!

How many computers have you seen today? There might be a computer in your house or classroom. People in your house may own a tablet or a mobile phone. Did you know, though, that there are also smaller computers inside some toys, games, TVs and microwaves?

People use computers every day, but what do computers actually do?

By the late 1970s, computers were small enough to use at school and work. The monitor only showed words and numbers, and only in one colour!

By 1990, computers were cheap enough for many people to have one at home. People could search for information and send emails, but more slowly than today.

Today, computers are everywhere!

Today

03 What do computers do?

Do you know all the names of everyone in your school? Probably not! It's hard for people to remember so many names, but this is easy for a computer. Computers work faster with numbers and remember more things than people can.

The information that computers store is called data. Data can be numbers, pictures, sounds or words.

04 What we put in

A computer needs data from us to be useful. It uses sensors to get information like how we see, hear and feel. Sensors turn what you do into data. Let's find some sensors on this computer!

A microphone hears what you say.

The trackpad feels where you move your finger.

These sensors are called inputs because they go into the computer.

A camera takes your picture.

A keyboard feels the keys you press to type.

05 What we get back

We've learnt that we can give computers information, but they can show us things, too. Can you see how this computer lets you see and hear?

The printer puts words and pictures onto paper.

These are called outputs, because they come out of the computer. Outputs turn data into pictures, words and sounds that you understand.

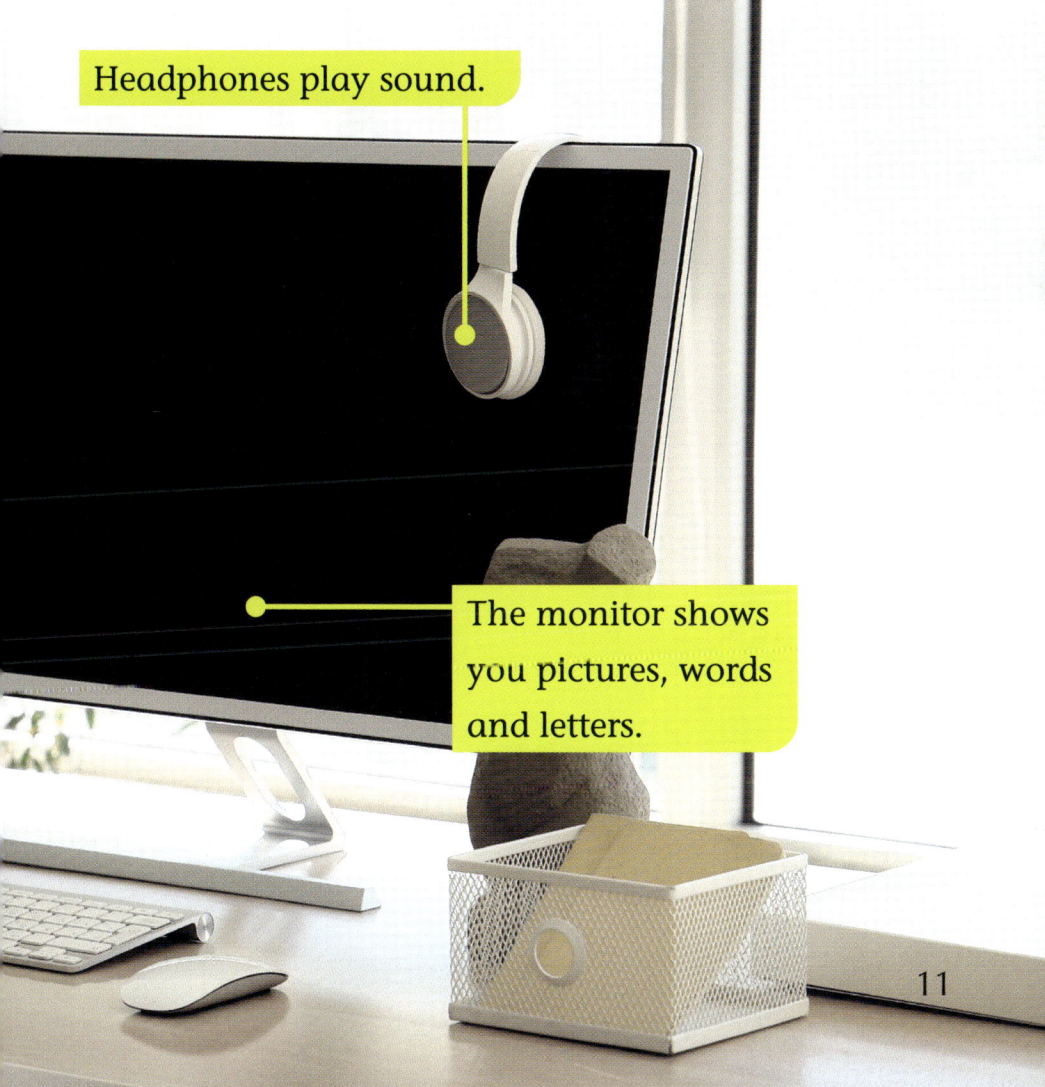

Headphones play sound.

The monitor shows you pictures, words and letters.

06 A computer's job

A computer's job is to process data. Processing means taking inputs, doing something useful, and then turning these into outputs. For example, you can put in two numbers and the computer will add them together for you and tell you the answer.

Can you find the processing on this video call?

Your video and sound goes into the computer.

Your computer changes the video and sound into numbers.

07 A computer's memory

Inside the computer is the Central Processing Unit (CPU). The CPU is where processing happens. It's a bit like our brains – taking information in, working with it and remembering it. A computer needs to remember data to process it, so it saves or stores the data to memory.

CPU

08 Bits and binary

A computer's memory is made up of 'bits' to store data. A bit is like a tiny switch – it's either ON or OFF. In computing, ON is 1 and OFF is 0. This means that computers can store data using only the numbers 0 and 1 – they don't use any other numbers! These are called binary numbers.

a computer's memory

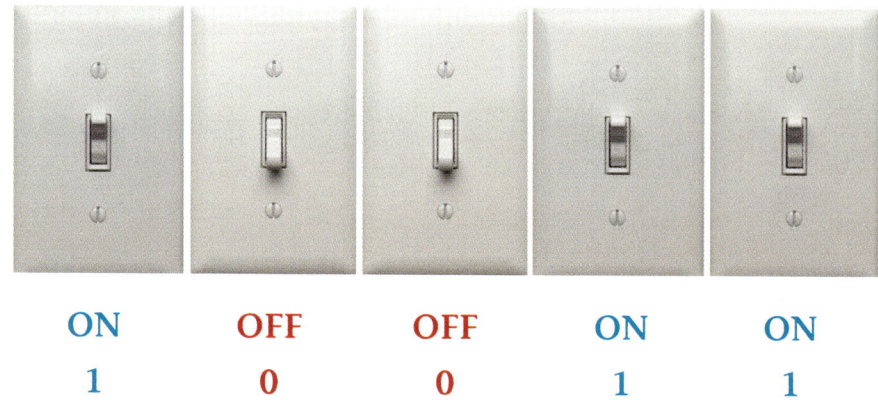

ON	OFF	OFF	ON	ON
1	0	0	1	1

0s and 1s don't meant much to us, but they mean something to the computer. The switches above are showing 10011 in binary – which is the number 19 to you!

The digital stopwatch uses the binary number 10011 in its memory, but shows you 19 on the screen.

09 Pictures are pixels

All pictures on a computer are made up of very small squares, called pixels. Every pixel has a colour, which is a number to the computer.

Binary numbers can be used to store anything in a computer's memory. We have already seen that they can mean numbers. They can also mean colours, sounds or words.

This is how a computer might store colours of pixels:

10 Algorithms and code

An algorithm is a set of instructions to solve a problem step-by-step. Can you write an algorithm to get the car to the blue square? One way is:

1 Go forward 3 squares

2 Turn right

3 Go forward 2 squares

Can you think of another way?

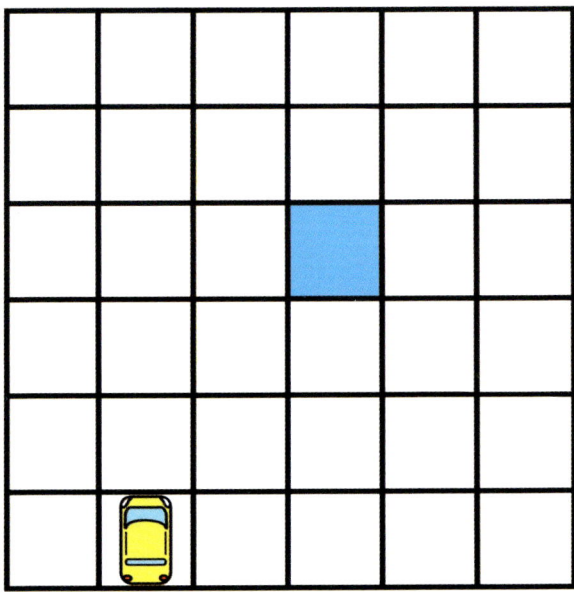

Computers do not understand words like people do. People write programs to tell the computer what to do and these programs are written in code. Both computers and people can understand code.

The code for moving the car to the blue square might look like this:

```
car.forward(3).turn(RIGHT).forward(2)
```

It tells the car to go forward, turn, then go forward again.

The numbers 3 and 2 say how far to go forward, and RIGHT says which way to turn. Full stops connect the car to the actions.

11 Saving files

When you use a program to save data, it is sometimes called a file. Each file has a name so it is easy to find. It's like putting a piece of paper in a folder so you can find it later.

The program tells the computer how to read the 0s and 1s in the file. Instead of 0s and 1s, you might see a photo from your camera or a typed-up letter.

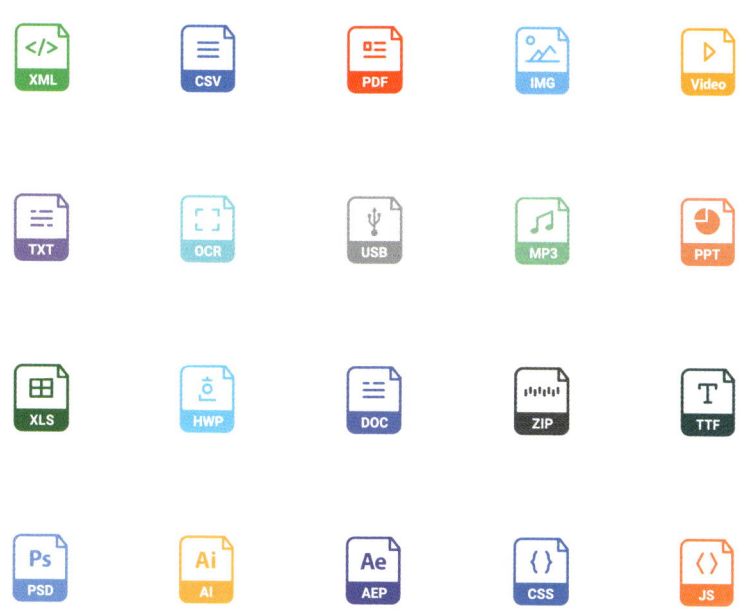

1 2 What is the internet?

The internet is how people with computers send files and data to each other. What do you like to do on the internet?

Look up information for your schoolwork on a website.

Buy things that are not in the nearby shops to be delivered to your home.

Find music to listen to using apps.

Send files, photos or emails.

Find films to watch using apps.

All of these are possible through computers sending 0s and 1s to each other!

13 Being safe on the internet

There are many interesting and important things to see and explore on the Internet, but it is also like a busy city. You must be careful of strangers or unexpected information. Make sure you have an adult you trust nearby, and don't give out any important details, like your name, your age or where you live.

14 Computers in the future

Artificial Intelligence, or AI for short, is a computer program that people can give many different kinds of problems to, and it will help with the problems. In the future, AI might help you with school work or in your job like a person can. AI can help with problems but does not truly understand them. We also need to check that what AI tells us is true.

Computers are still changing and improving. Over time they have become smaller, faster and a bigger part of our lives. Many people use computers and the internet at school or at work. Some people have jobs designing and building computers and writing programs. Now you know a little bit about how a computer works, too!

How computers work

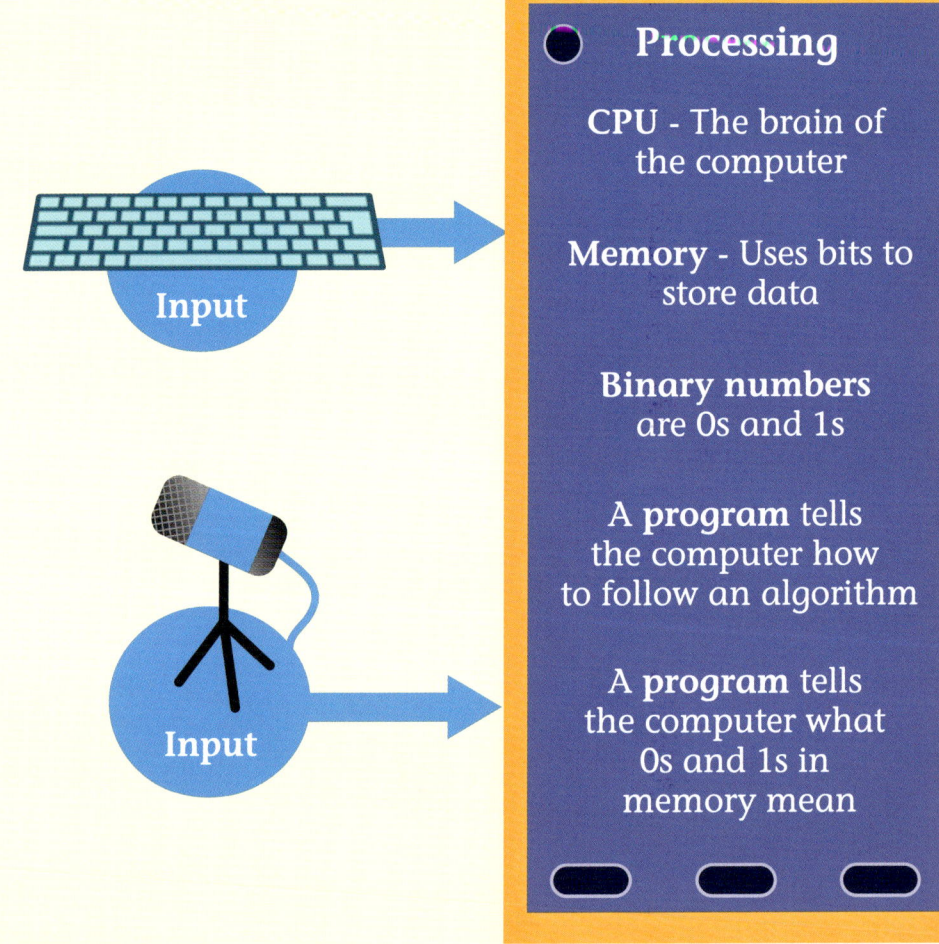

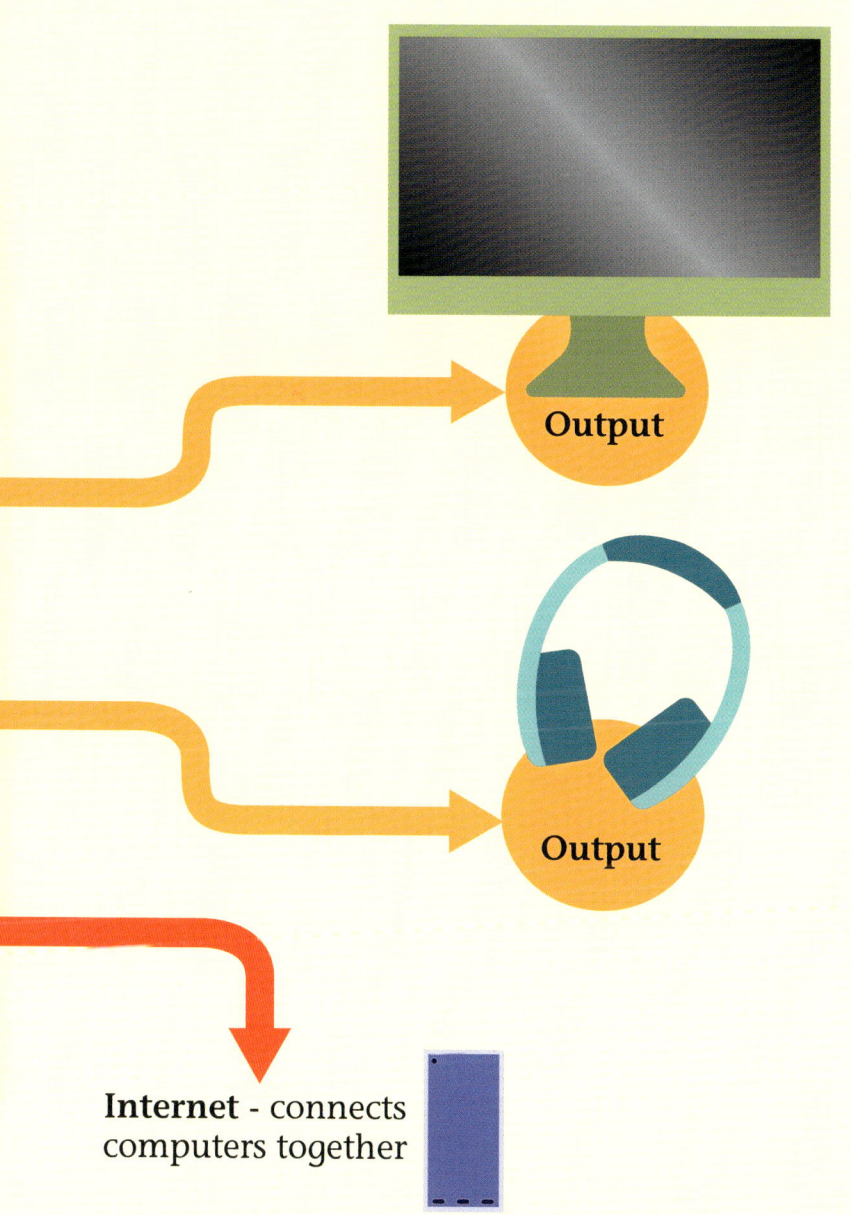

Ideas for reading

Written by Gill Matthews
Primary Literacy Consultant

Reading objectives:
- be introduced to non-fiction books that are structured in different ways
- discuss and clarify the meanings of words, linking new meanings to known vocabulary
- draw on what they already know or on background information and vocabulary provided by the teacher
- answer and ask questions

Spoken language objectives:
- use relevant strategies to build their vocabulary
- participate in discussions, presentations, performances, role play, improvisations and debates

Curriculum links: Relationships education: Online relationships
Interest words: interesting, important, stranger, unexpected
Word count: 1250

Build a context for reading
- Ask children to look at the front cover of the book and to read the title.
- Discuss what kind of book they think this is and what they will find out from it.
- Read the back cover blurb. Confirm that this is an information book.
- Explore what children know about computers and what they use them for.

Understand and apply reading strategies
- Ask children to find the contents page. Discuss the purpose and organisation of a contents list.
- Ask them to use the contents to find Chapter 1.
- Read pp2–3 aloud and discuss the questions that are asked.